Take-Home Animal Rhymes

by

DR. MARY MANZ SIMON

illustrated by
Ron Kauffman

Carson-Dellosa Christian Publishing
Greensboro, North Carolina

Table of Contents

Making the Books

Many reproducible books involve complicated copying, folding, and cutting. However, *Take-Home Animal Rhymes* pays special attention to ease of use for children and busy teachers. First, make one-sided copies of the pages. Take care to place each page in the center of the photocopying space rather than flush against the edge.

Have the student color each page of the book, then have her cut the pages in half on the dashed lines. (Coloring before cutting and binding makes the coloring easier.) Finally, have each child turn the pages in the same direction, check that they are in the correct order, and staple them on the left side. Help students with stapling so that their books open easily. Students can also bind the pages using a hole punch and yarn or metal rings.

Credits

Author ....Dr. Mary Manz Simon
Editor ....Carol Layton
Layout Design......................Mark Conrad
Art Coordinators ....Julie Kinlaw, Jon Nawrocik
Inside Illustrations...............Ron Kauffman
Cover Design.......................Annette Hollister-Papp
Cover Illustration ....Ron Kauffman

Printed in the USA • All rights reserved.   ISBN 1-59441-292-8

To the Adult

How do children learn Christian character? These core beliefs are both caught and taught. Use the making of these mini-books to trigger discussions about what it means to live a godly life.

Bees (helpfulness)

During the early years, a child needs nonstop assistance. Those caring for a child need help, too. Although adults might feel uncomfortable asking for help, honestly admitting our need is a sign of strength. What a blessing that we can confidently say with the psalmist, *"We depend on you, LORD, to help and protect us."* (Psalm 33:20)

Bunny (love)

It's easy to love when everything is going well; it's hard to show love when a child is acting willfully. As we mature in our relationship with God, we find that God continues to love us—even when we act willfully. We are reminded that God's extreme love for us enables us to lovingly discipline a willful child. (1 John 4:19)

Elephant (gentleness)

God made one of the largest animals capable of gentleness. An elephant not only can lift heavy logs, but, as the mini-book suggests (page 14), its flexible trunk can also handle a delicate flower. When we face difficult situations with a small child, it is easy to let our size dominate. But, like the elephant, we can show gentleness. As St. Paul reminds us, *"Be faithful, loving, dependable, and gentle."* (1 Timothy 6:11)

Froggie (honesty)

One developmental task during the preschool years is to distinguish between truth and falsehood. That's why it's helpful to clarify between real and make-believe as the opportunity arises. For example: "You played kitchen this morning at school and now you are helping to make a real sandwich." Because a young child flips back and forth between the imaginative world of play and the real world of life, he needs time and patience to learn what's true and what's false.

Billy Goat (obedience)

A child may find it difficult to learn obedience, and adults may have even more trouble teaching it. After all, enforcing rules isn't always easy or fun—a child might have a tantrum when rules are enforced. Yet learning to live by and enforce rules is important for children and adults. Children who are allowed to live outside the rules can be uncertain about what is right and wrong. To review God's rules, see Exodus 20:3-17.

Hummingbird (trust)

When a baby learns to trust in others, she develops a foundation for building relationships throughout life. Children learn they can count on some people and observe that others disappoint them. "Trust in the Lord" is repeated throughout Scripture. That's a message we also need to repeat to ourselves as we accompany a child through the seasons of life.

Kitty (cleanliness)

Cleanliness may be next to godliness, but that's neither scriptural nor does it reflect the typical state of children. Yet, taking care of ourselves is important. St. Paul reminds us that *". . . you are God's temple and that his Spirit lives in you."* (1 Corinthians 3:16) Generations of parents have encouraged children to wash away germs. Today's parents are also challenged to guard their children's hearts from unclean influences in our culture.

Lion (respect)

The lack of respect in today's entertainment culture causes adults to feel a sense of urgency to teach children this virtue. A respectful attitude will develop only with repeated teaching. We must continually model respect for others, for God, and for His commandments. As St. Peter states, we should *"Respect everyone. . . ."* (1 Peter 2:17)

Monkey (forgiveness)

Learning to forgive and forget can be easier for a child than for an adult. After all, a child goes quickly from one person to another, flitting between activities. Yet, we might remember the little and the big things that hurt us. We might forgive on a mental level but find it hard to do so on an emotional level. Even so, to forgive and be forgiven creates a cleansing unlike any other. (Colossians 3:13)

Owl (wisdom)

The ability to make wise choices is necessary for children growing up in a world filled with options. We begin teaching this skill by asking a toddler if he wants to wear the red or blue shirt and then moving on to more challenging decisions. A wise person makes one decision every day: to pray for a child.

Penguin (courtesy)

Do children today lack good manners? Some social historians note that the lack of etiquette, or simply common-sense politeness, is a by-product of living at hyper speed. Being courteous and kind often doesn't take more time: it takes practice. The words of Proverbs 16:21 offer a timely reminder for all who work with children: *". . . if you speak kindly, you can teach others."*

Puppy (friendliness)

Childhood friendships come and go, as children move between seasons, activities, and classes. And yet, as children grow up, we must continually help them work through social issues. Friendship is a true blessing not to be taken for granted. (Proverbs 17:17) Like all relationships, investing in people takes work, but the benefits, even for a young child, are enormous.

Sheep (patience)

Patience does not come naturally to children. They must gradually learn to be patient. We can help children by keeping our expectations realistic, modeling patience, and affirming times when they wait without fussing. We can also pray that the Holy Spirit will work in the child to give her patience, along with the other fruit of the Spirit. (Galatians 5:22-23)

Spider (creativity)

When we find a crayon mark on the wall or leftovers artistically mashed together on the dinner plate, we might wish a child had less creativity. And yet, the ability to think spontaneously and act with flexibility adds continuing freshness and newness to life. Mirroring their insights, innocence, and creativity are advantages of being around young children. Jesus reminds us that *"People who are like these children belong to God's kingdom."* (Luke 18:16)

Turtle (determination)

Willpower feeds determination —a quality essential in those who work with children. After all, when working with children, closure seems so far away: Will that child ever learn to zip a jacket? Will he ever write his name? Sometimes, we must force ourselves to work alongside a child for many months before he acquires a skill. Yet life's irritations that seem so major today, fade when we refocus on what really matters in life. "Major in the majors," adults tell children. That's a good reminder for us, too. We want to say with St. Paul in his personal letter to his "dear" Timothy, *"I have finished the race, and I have been faithful."* (2 Timothy 4:7)

ASK THE BEES!
A Lesson in Helpfulness

CD-204022 *Take-Home Animal Rhymes*

Worker bees are buzzing 'round,
flying high above the ground.

Find some food to feed queen bee.
Guard the entrance to the tree.

2

Fan your wings to cool the hive:
keep those other bees alive.

3

You are called a worker bee
and the reason's clear to me.

4

You help ev'ry day and night
making sure that all is right.

5

Here's a lesson straight from you:
we can help each other, too.

6

. . . each helps
the other. . . .

Isaiah 41:6 NIV

The wings of a worker bee move more than 11,000 times each minute.
That's what makes the buzzing sound when a bee flies by.
We know the worker bee is called that because she's busy helping others.
Do you work so hard that people call you a "worker child"?

7

ASK THE BUNNY!

A Lesson in Love

CD-204022 *Take-Home Animal Rhymes*

Bunny, I will keep you warm.
I will keep you safe from harm.

1

I so like your floppy ear.
I love you, my bunny dear.

2

And because I love you so,
I will give you food to grow.

3

I will find fresh clover, too;
that is part of loving you.

4

I hug you to show I care,
for you are my little hare.

5

I am grateful you are here.
Thank you, God, for bunny dear.

6

God is love.   1 John 4:16

There are many ways to show love: you can kiss, hug, do a kind deed,
or give someone a compliment. How will you show love today?

7

ASK THE ELEPHANT!

A Lesson in Gentleness

CD-204022 *Take-Home Animal Rhymes*

Elephant with trunk so long,
elephant with body strong,

1

I have seen you in the zoo.
I know you are gentle, too.

2

"Here's a flower picked for you.
That is something I can do."

3

I want to be gentle, too.
What do you think I should do?

4

"Touching softly, being kind,
showing that you always mind."

5

"Gentle thoughts will make you grin
when your heart shows from within."

6

Always be gentle
with others.

Philippians 4:5

Speaking softly, touching kindly, and holding carefully are all parts of being gentle.
When did you show gentleness recently?

7

ASK THE FROGGIE!

A Lesson in Honesty

CD-204022 *Take-Home Animal Rhymes*

Froggie, froggie, jump so high,
Did you catch that little fly?

1

"No, I missed it. See it go?
I was just a little slow."

Froggie, I am proud of you.
Being truthful's hard to do.

"Yes, but I won't tell a lie,
even if I miss that fly."

4

"If someday, I fibbed to you,
you might wonder, 'Is that true?'"

5

"But when I speak honestly,
then you always can trust me."

6

I always speak
the truth and
refuse to tell a lie.

Proverbs 8:7

Sometimes, you might mix up what's real and what's just pretend.
But now that you are growing up, it's easier to know what's real, or true.
If you need a reminder to be honest, ask God for help.

7

ASK THE BILLY GOAT!

A Lesson in Obedience

CD-204022 *Take-Home Animal Rhymes*

Billy goat, you must obey.
You must stay inside today.

1

Stay right here, just as you should.
Rules are made for your own good.

Even if I go away,
I expect you to obey.

"But I want to chew the gate.
and I want to stay up late."

4

That would not be good for you.
Rules show what is right to do.

5

Follow rules and you will stay
safe and happy every day.

We show our love
for God by
obeying his
commandments. . . .

1 John 5:3

Do you agree with what it says in this little book—
"rules are made for your own good"? That's true, you know.
People who love and care for you make rules to keep you healthy and safe.
Will you think about this the next time you feel like being disobedient?

ASK THE HUMMINGBIRD!

A Lesson in Trust

CD-204022 *Take-Home Animal Rhymes*

Hummingbird, you fly so fast.
One quick look and then you're past.

1

Little bird, don't you feel fear
when big birds come very near?

"Oh, no, God created me,
so I was made perfectly."

"I can fly across the sea,
I have confidence you see."

4

"God gives us the things we need.
We can trust him, yes, indeed."

5

"I can count on God, it's true.
Don't you know that you can, too?"

6

Trust the
LORD, and he
will help you.

Proverbs 20:22

It's hard to count on somebody who has disappointed you.
Even people we love let us down, but God doesn't.
You can always trust God.

7

ASK THE KITTY!

A Lesson in Cleanliness

CD-204022 *Take-Home Animal Rhymes*

Kitty, kitty, oh so clean,
cleanest I have ever seen.

1

As I watch you groom your fur,
I can sometimes hear you purr.

2

I wash ev'ry single day,
to keep nasty germs away.

3

Even if I'm in a rush,
I will stop and use the brush.

4

Kitty, careful, here's the broom,
now I need to clean my room.

5

You don't need to bathe like me.
Your coat cleans just perfectly!

6

Wash me clean
from all of my
sin and guilt.

Psalm 51:2

Have you ever sniffed your hands after washing with soap and water?
Or smelled clean clothes when they come out of a dryer?
We can clean our hands and clothes, but Jesus washes away all
our messy mistakes. He gives the best kind of clean!

7

ASK THE LION!
A Lesson in Respect

CD-204022 *Take-Home Animal Rhymes*

Lion, tell me why it's true,
others show respect to you.

1

Is it that you're jungle king?
Or is it some other thing?

2

"I respect the others here.
I treat all with love and care."

3

"Everyone has dignity
from the zebra to the flea."

4

"Kindly say and kindly do,
others then will value you."

5

"When you honor all you see,
then you act respectfully."

6

Respect
everyone. . . .

1 Peter 2:17

Respect isn't a big word, but it's a big idea. When you respect someone,
you treat them like you want to be treated. Do you want people to be kind?
Treat them kindly. Do you want people to listen to you?
Listen to others. These are ways you show respect.

7

ASK THE MONKEY!

A Lesson in Forgiveness

CD-204022 *Take-Home Animal Rhymes*

Monkey, monkey, in the tree,
why did you toss that at me?

1

"I just wasn't acting wise.
Let me now apologize."

2

"When I say, 'Oh pardon me,'
inside I feel clean and free."

3

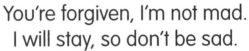
You're forgiven, I'm not mad.
I will stay, so don't be sad.

4

"Thank you for forgiving me
when I hit you with that tree."

5

"Saying 'I am sorry,' too,
is what God wants us to do."

6

Forgive us for
doing wrong,
as we
forgive others.

Matthew 6:12

You may find it easy to say the words, "I forgive you."
However, you may find it hard to actually forgive someone in your heart.
God forgives us, even when we do very bad things.
Because God forgives us, we can forgive others, even when it's hard to do.

7

ASK THE OWL!
A Lesson in Wisdom

CD-204022 *Take-Home Animal Rhymes*

Owl hooting in the tree,
what words do you have for me?

1

"Use the gifts God gives to you.
Think about all you can do."

2

Wise old owl, don't fly away,
What else do you have to say?

3

"Choose to share your loving heart.
Wisdom's more than being smart."

4

"You must listen, God will lead.
He gives wisdom that you need."

5

"Wisdom is a gift, it's true,
and that's something God gives you."

6

Listen carefully to
my instructions,
and you will be wise.

Proverbs 8:33

It's not always easy to make the right choice.
Sometimes, there is more than one way to do something right.
Ask God to help you to be wise.

7

ASK THE PENGUIN!
A Lesson in Courtesy

CD-204022 *Take-Home Animal Rhymes*

Penguin, you look so polite—
dressed up in your black and white.

1

When you stand so tall and pose,
do your manners match your clothes?

2

"Yes, we penguins gather tight
to survive a frigid night."

3

"That is simply kind you know,
when there is such ice and snow."

4

"And we take turns at the nest
so we all can eat and rest."

5

"Saying 'please' and 'I thank you' shows you have good manners, too."

6

Kind words are like honey—they cheer you up and make you feel strong.

Proverbs 16:24

Do you have good manners?
Saying "please," and "thank you," shows that you have good manners.
People will say you are courteous—and that is a good thing to be!

7

ASK THE PUPPY!

A Lesson in Friendliness

CD-204022 *Take-Home Animal Rhymes*

Puppy, puppy, come and stay,
for I need a friend today.

1

If I'm sad or feeling blue,
I can always count on you.

2

When I see your wagging tail,
I feel better, without fail.

3

Friends will share the good and bad.
Friends stay near when you are sad.

4

Friends will care in good times, too;
they can have such fun with you.

5

You are such a friend it's true:
I am so glad God made you.

6

A friend loves
at all times. . . .

Proverbs 17:17 NIV

Who is your best friend? If your friend doesn't know
that Jesus loves him, tell him. Sharing the love of Jesus
is the most important thing we can do for a friend.

7

ASK THE SHEEP!

A Lesson in Patience

CD-204022 *Take-Home Animal Rhymes*

Woolly, Woolly, please stand there
while we start to shear your hair.

1

You look like a great big sheep,
with your fleece so thick and deep.

2

Soon you will feel nice and cool.
Just be patient, that's the rule.

3

Patience means you have to wait,
even if it's getting late.

4

When you're calm and do not fuss,
good things come to both of us.

5

Since you stood so patiently,
your wool made a coat for me!

6

It's wise to be patient. . . .

Proverbs 19:11

When you have trouble waiting, talk to God.
Simply pray, "Lord, help me be patient." He will hear you and help you.

7

ASK THE SPIDER!

A Lesson in Creativity

CD-204022 *Take-Home Animal Rhymes*

Spider spinning a new web,
back and forth around my head.

1

There is nothing when you start,
now your web's a work of art.

2

God made you to weave in air:
creativity to share.

3

I can be creative, too.
I can make things, just like you.

4

While you spin, I'll sing and play.
I do things in my own way.

5

God has gifted you and me
with great creativity!

6

Everything God
created is good.

1 Timothy 4:4

Do you like to draw? To sing? To run very fast?
You draw pictures, sing songs, and run races in your own special way.
That's because God has made you special.
No one draws pictures, sings songs, or runs races exactly like you!

7

ASK THE TURTLE!
A Lesson in Determination

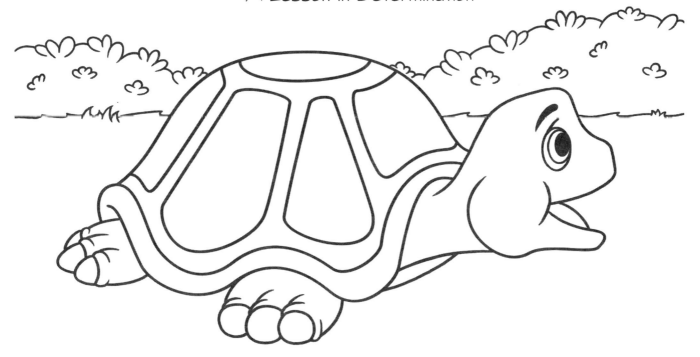

CD-204022 *Take-Home Animal Rhymes*

Turtle moving very slow,
staying near the ground so low.

1

Turtle, what can you teach me?
What's the lesson I should see?

2

"When I want to cross the yard,
I know that the task is hard."

3

"Then, I move at my own pace
although I won't win a race."

4

"Taking one step at a time,
I know I will be just fine."

5

"So what will I say to you?
Don't give up till you are through!"

6

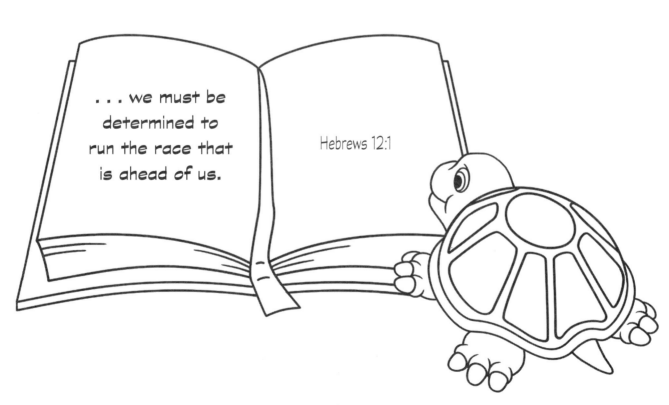

. . . we must be determined to run the race that is ahead of us.

Hebrews 12:1

It's easy to give up when a job is tough.
When you need help to finish what you start, ask God for help.

7